ASK AGAIN LATER

A S K
AGAIN
LATER

Nancy White

Tiger Bark Press * Rochester, New York * 2017

Published by
TIGER BARK PRESS
202 Mildorf Avenue
Rochester, NY 14609

Tiger Bark Press books are published by Steven Huff.
Photographs by Kirby Vaillant-White.

ISBN: 978-0-9976305-5-8

This publication made possible with funding
from the New York State Council on the Arts
with the support of Governor Andrew M. Cuomo
and the New York State Legislature.

*For Patricia and Patricia
and Ruth*

*In memory of Helen Harmon Corbin
June 2, 1908 – June 11, 1993*

CONTENTS

III Lost Character

IV Castaways

NOA

She stumped us, the flinty
glitter of her tale,
her koans blunt and rubbly.

What to call her, how
to explain? And no one asks
for her anyway.

One more bird by the side of the road,
a high note dropped when
we just can't hit it.

I

Overboard

RUTH AT THE WELL

Sisters, I promise you a lair inviolable.
(The cup is larger than our thirst. In your hands

it's warm, size of a fox's lung.) Like us,
the desert is dissolving, is time

ground down slowly. All travel
tangential or blind, every one of us far

from home. In one word our ghosts
are swarming. (Take it, the vessel's not heavy

though chipped and rough.) Recognize:
your words press back against the desert,

and the heat against our backs, our feet,
the ruts, belongs to us.

JAEL

Cheek against a flank—
the she-herd waiting as patiently
as goats can wait—I felt her milk drop,
the musky scent better than flowers. But
here came Sisera weary and stubborn, already

planning his return through the pass, and
after him another army, lead by Deborah
the mad and Barak the simple.
I gave him milk and let him rest in my bed.
A stupid man, but my neighbor once, and twice

he'd fixed my loom. He heard their iron wheels
or felt the tremor of the ground, rushed
out and tripped, flew headlong onto the tent-peg
there and was dead. Barak rode up, and Deb
all crazy-eyed at his side began to rant,

Jael, our savior! Brave Jael has slain him
as he slept! My goats ran off bleating
at the din. It took a week to track and
tether them together, bring them home. Three
I lost. Two miscarried. That made nine.

TO ESTHER

It's just…the way you eat it raw,
when time, my lost sister,
is like the rare persimmon, how
you have to wait—remember?—till it practically

rots. To get a green one down, you need
salt or to be as cooked, part-man, as you.
But then (I can't forget the days together)
you play the strings with strong fingers, exempt

from our girlie-girlie rules. Surprising,
but some of us have loaded apron
pockets up with stones. Look… It doesn't help
that you strum verse for the judges

while we wear your child's white
spit-up like a lying badge of peace. But (loves,
will we slay the bitch in haste? What was
she to do?) your lute did once play true.

JONAH

I can't remember, not the way you heard.
Trials, but that you know yourself…
Sit here in the shade, let me see that hand.
I have an ointment. Such curiosities,
wherever I went. There was a girl,
eyes as dark as dates, with that golden shade?
She lifted a hand and pulled me near…
Do you know, I still smell her, spiced
and dangerful. She's one of the jewels
of my old mind. They ask about the whale,
travelers want that story, and I do recall
an island, a dull life really. That tiny spring,
never faltering, it saved me. Hot wind, and a reek
of seaweed rotting in the bay, I remember
fear—but a fishing boat found me,
and I helped them haul their heavy nets. How
the silver spilled up from the generous sea!
They dressed me like a son, a thick robe,
russet with a jaunty yellow hem. For certain,
the loveliness of strangers—a life like mine
will show you that, again and again.

REBEKAH

I walked where you directed.
Drank the story. Counted the beads of it.
But Mother, the conniving! Our
tribal skirmishes quaint by comparison.
Among brothers, son to father, mother to son—
then they hold to the result like honor.

The prize stolen back and forth
like some sharp fork. Who
can tell them apart in the end? Isaac left
both sons unleavened. I came across that desert
thinking He was sending me.

I bear their sons, nurse
their daughters, spin the wild
goatswool… The robes I weave are white,
wiry to the touch. I myself feed and
clothe them, my own work twins
the men like lambs. Who
could go home after this?

HOLOFERNES

We come to our final wager.
Why not lie in the grass and rest first,
let white petals from the almond tree
coast across your skin and away. In another
story I would sing to you. Forget that thirst

to do our will and the power of the body
that defines us, makes us such fine
specimens. It turns out this life's quick
and lonely, and soot smears suddenly
on our deeds... But have you noticed?

God forgives the victor. How alike
our stubbornness, and the cowards
we lead. In another story I'd stay home
for the sound of one woman sleeping.
Dawn's coming. Let it be clean.

ESTHER ADVISES

coil down quiet
among their customs
curl past the dead

wives into the
daughters' pockets
quick as cleopatra's

tiny curse: slide: water
pressing down
stones under

the unsurprisable
sun open your
mind your legs

your bales of cloth
fear is the next meal
always the caravan off

without you your
aunt dying mordechai's
name on her lips pet

the harem girls to
fatten their love who
will pay for you who

could ever pay enough

ON SETTING HER FREE

Between us we made one pious bride,
then dutiful wife. On and on, this execution,
and his wealth made it bearable to sit or stroll
commendably. I didn't think about the burden,
not until the army came, till the elders said,
In five days we surrender. Who were they
to give away our grain, the children

into slavery again? Of the six? Two
were suitors to my widowhood, their eyes
across the table flickering. She knew, she
saw it rise in me. She says boredom had grown
choking, but I say anger snapped my filigreed
obedience. I called for the scarves and skirts
of my marriage, ones my husband liked.

Dance for me, he'd say. I felt a fool
swaying my hips, couldn't look him in the eye.
To untie me was the work of a minute,
his stuttering small soft hands…
But when the chosen robes clung to me again
and shimmered, I was shaming no children,
only my village, which had abandoned us all.

So we combed and painted. Hair
glinting in the sun unbound, I said to the council,
You know me by name. Give me the five days.
Their gaze crawled after me, down to the enemy tents.
She knows the truth is we ran out of wine and still
he looked at me like a general. But finally he slept…
How easy it was—two swings of the blade, one

for the breath in him, asleep, and then the spine.
He hardly made a sound, even less
than when he finished between my thighs. She
came—the empty bag, a cloth—and took
my cold hand. She carried him. She waited
through words and words, the council,
brought me home to that house, the sound

of boys playing, afternoons of hot light.
I gave her up, who bore the bagged and bloody deed,
who veiled my appetite and lies. She wept
when she covered his face—I won't forget—
and bowed her head to his guards. I remember
she left behind our sash and the gold bangles.
My steady one. I freed her. As if she were mine.

MOSES

I stumbled back
with his name
like a beating heart
my hands hurt and

heavy I tell you I felt
his voice
strike like a fang
burn in me

the flood stung
me words
drowned wrung me
dry flung from

the living
rent   exact
hear it   no second
chance no   mercy these
rules   these only
            they

LOT'S WIFE

We're staying, he said. *My business
prospers, we have sons.* That city
where I was pulled behind the stalls
and held facedown on a sack of grain,
where the women whispered.

They showed how to soften the hard
grain, to sew those hides so tough
my needles bent. A warning their one
weapon: *The men are meeting tonight.*
I'd bar my daughters in, feign sleep.

When the travelers came, their beauty a foul
perfume along the streets, the men grew hard
and wild. My husband, still the foreigner,
offered our girls instead, went into the alley
to give them away. He said, *But I knew*

they were angels of the lord! Each year
I understood him less. He pleaded,
I'll find a village in the hills, and traded my girls
for an ass so he could ride faster from that place he
chose. I followed but the ragged herder said,

Get away, old woman. He leashed them
to his saddle horn and they were gone. Nothing left
but ugly sky, sand barren as salt. Days I'd labored,
minutes loved: burned off. I made no mark
on this world, its angels as bad as its men.

NOAH

It was illusion, you know, the water—
I realized much later. We drifted, some docile,
some going mad with it, the smell of dust washing
over us. Eventually a ragged starling (or a dove)
landed on the deck where we were strewn

in the heat, caught in its claw a shred—
green. We declared an end: salvation!
The ramp dropped and beasts departed, most
not knowing what hit them, just glad to taste
spring creeping up from the ground.

If it weren't for the stories I might not
believe there was a boat. And stories we pass
back and forth so their edges fray, words soft
as dust. Or who's going to say the story
isn't the island, with us drifting by.

RUTH TO HER DAUGHTER

Remember the old music master and his tuning pipes?
He had two notes, would start us off…
Those days no one could write a ticket out,
even Boaz with his baskets and baskets of grain.
The way it never occurred to them? I continue
to find that beautiful. Most of the time
I was like the corn itself, was their
unspoken word. I found music in that.
It was enough. But not for you.

II

Do Over

IN BETHLEHEM

flesh burst no wish
left her skin burns
hums drummed overcoming banks and the heat's
a skin against
the hours against skull belly flank calf heel into
the ear a belling into

the new blank her cry
salt on lips in mouth like truth unbearable born

she lifts
the afterbirth in both hands
heavy meaty trophy the antilight blood
now down her arms like ribbons like brands
someone takes it from her takes what is done hands
her all that's yet to bear

NEW IN TOWN

Yes, he drops by, still for no reason. Even
today when rain bathes the house and
the path sheds its glove of dust.

He's going on again, *The hydrogen*
molecule clings to oxygen:
but we have learned

the two will never really touch. It wasn't me,
but his story got around, how he fled
when his father's voice

beat him like a stick, when the words
scoured him down, till his skin
soured, till his hair

and mouth and eyes flamed. Arriving, he told us,
My father's dead, later, *I have no father,*
then, *I am the son of God.*

We are a garden, he says. *We will grow again.*
My holy father promises. Go ahead
and laugh but with my own eyes

I see the lily lean to him, the cranesbill weep
as he sits on the back steps drinking
a glass of water from my house.

CHRIST EXPLAINS HIS YOUTH

Nothing felt so important as getting
inside. I was fucking them. Get under
the skirt, jeans, whatever. But get
it, inside, make yourself
felt, you know, so I could see it
in her face, what it was

for her. I mean, it wasn't always
what she wanted, exactly, but
I'm not saying they didn't let
me. They always let me. That's
what was so weird, what were
they feeling?

Not that it mattered to me
back then. Not at the time. You
see what I'm saying, half
of me was tuned out, all
the way to the nothing at
the end of the dial.

I had nothing to say
but I wanted to see
their faces, wanted to push
back the closed eyelids and see
inside. Fucking, I used
each face like it was a meter

attached by a wire to what I was
down there, in that jerking
lever I urged like a car toward a wreck,

wanting smoke, the roar,
wanting to feel myself
running from the crash, on fire.

MAGDALENE

this is the sweeter fruit eaten
in sleep the black
& wilder mane

the dream-mare cracks around her
cresting another night our only
job to love what blooms

from these portholes our bodies
we turn at the blue center
like captive fish radiant

in our tank we brush something
large & crowning   salute
just lucky

APPLICANT

You alone must
coat the ceiling white.
Don't drip or spill the paint.
You must leave no rings, will
cease the murder in your face,
must learn to make sweet coffee
and surrender without asking us to.
Feed our breath and with your body
bless the roots of salt marshes, preparing
the world to stay as it is. You are the first
who will fall to silence. Let the others speak.
You must love our clumsiest craven touch.
The gap dubbed history must be redeemed
by your gentleness, your elevating heat.
You will not take credit. You will give it
all away. Come be our Christ for here we
lie too bright and broken to be spared.
Want nothing. Be sufficient, done,
and when we hang from the cliff
by our last fingers, you
let go first.

JUST A NEIGHBOR

After a rain, we'd sit by the waterfall…
little things he did like a woman:
tuck up his robe, shade his eyes to watch
a bird, touch your arm. When the crowd saw
devils stream out, not love, not relief
and the sky spilling through me, he said,

We see what inhabits the eye. He worked
the bread with us sometimes, humming…
Children shouting in the street didn't trouble him.
When he rose, we saw a mother returning
from the many deaths of childbirth,
blood on her thighs and hands, her breasts hardening,

the next life in her arms. We knew the ways
they'd want to break him. They couldn't guess why
they trembled. When he bent to lace a sandal,
they said, *brother,* or *Lord.* Because he led, he
commanded, they couldn't see they loved him like
a woman and that like a woman he loved them.

MARY MAGDALENE TO JESUS

The doorway a woman,
your body
Her

vessel. I
saved you, you heard
Her name and we were the halls

and gullies of Her ear. Only one
direction then, swimming
the curl. You were

made in Her delight—yet
what you brought
the men

later bore
no ease, bore scant
resemblance in the end.

MARTHA ADMITS SHE WAS ANGRY

Easy for him to say, with her long hair
brushing his feet for the first time, hair
I had combed and scented with the crushed
river lilies, the yellow and white.
She a little smitten, him smiling and

sure. Of course he was the son of God.
Meanwhile her bread rose too high,
the fire (it was her turn) sank low,
and the usual children stood at the door,
waiting. Words and words—good

enough, but still, what's a friend who
can't talk and shell beans at the same time?
Sister—I know that wish to sit absolutely still.
Harder to forgive the visitor assuming his
dinner would be prompt. I fed the fire,

set her bread. I gave the children milk and
heard their tale—a stranger pulled many days
dead from the water. Mostly I heard
his message anyhow, promises ringing
down the steps. He was always loud enough.

CHRIST TO GALILEE

you raised   me drove me asked
I be music   instead of hunger
in the rage   of tumbling cities
in salt plains   you still hear a passage
I did not want   your daughters
I wanted your   soft throats
wanted just half   the blood in your bodies and to
convince that   you must fail but still we're changing
I think   you're getting through
to Him   breathing singing accidental
tears   you tinge the air with breath or word
He   begins to recognize

JUDAS

you think I wanted this
story I didn't not wreck
not plummet
I loved his crazy ass but
I knew

one more teaspoon
of that magic could've
nursed us
a little longer though
this is all we

get

don't pity

yourself the spiral
of Roman smoke as blue
and wrong as
anything but that doesn't
make him

right don't
hang your short time
over that cold hook the hereafter
look around look and
remember I had my use

JOSEPH'S FIRST WIFE

I saw him at the market,
scalp thin, a bent old man.
They destroyed that boy he did

it for… He's done. A good price
for my weaving now. I'm safe.
But I want to know

if he still believes? *She was
a virgin, she was!* I wanted him back—
his youngest self—or not

to have loved a fool in the first place, to forget
the nights he bounced above me. Let him
feel the bite of blanked

paternity, how stupid now
and cold his sacrifice. I hate
what's left is the story,

still about
my failure though his is
the empty house.

DISCIPLE, TANGIERS

that light kept me a year in its grip
first my feet caught fire then my blood

we moved along the edge of endlessness
handless mouthless mindless

sand and ripe figs a night
on the rug with high merciless

stars in our mouths drank
brackish water the camel milk

learned to swim the afterness
to relinquish to lift knowing away

drift like ash like this land rising
to vanish vanishing to rise

LUCIFER ON TRUTH

but it hovers it gulps and grinds
like a black hole a scotch and soda

god's right to hide me
and you too but what if

truth could come previously
be obvious nourishing fruit

our skin warm and furred
oh god worries at the window

and the dark's piling deeper but
what if what if what if he's still wrong?

III

Lost Character

HOLE NO HOLE

because my hand must be one or the other
because the rattle in my lungs
because in me a bomb a leaf unfurling

ten then eleven then twelve
and blood is drying on my arms

because love nor needles seal us
days come like weather riding up the body
because I see it now all of it everywhere

and still there is a hole in my name

BETWEEN TESTAMENTS

I want my tribes to vanish, the faces
in a heavy tide rush away. No sound
but the void softly turning.
Without weather. No sky to hide in,
no soil souring, no stain… Lighter
than a frond against my skin, just breath,
the world unwound. Anything I do make
will be so small even I won't be able to see it.
Hissing like sand through the dark, I
will move particulate, precise as justice
and wide, before law, before error.

GOD AWOKE IN THE GARDEN

That was the day I sat up
and couldn't make out where
I was. The wall looked familiar
but not the sky, it seemed so empty,
and I wasn't alone. In this new place

rabbits barked and birds slithered, fruit
bloomed among the roots of trees.
I couldn't remember my name although yes
I was aware of searching… A woman lay
beside me, her eyes dark and easy with sleep,

then her hands reached to me, the first touch
a jolt unnameable: bliss? pain? *Shh*, she said then,
seeing my eyes move like birds, like rabbits,
afraid of the air that towered above me,
charging me so mighty, crushing me small.

GOD FINDS THE SAME PLACE TWICE

I know this place. The grassy bank
sagging, and the silky shuffle of gravel,
how hemlocks anchor the planet. This place…
peace after falling. The dappling leaves lap
our backs. The sun's lower, warmer,
a hint of pity in the air, but I'm telling you
I know those slabs, slaty, solid, tipping everything
to the sea. The same rope swings from the same
muttering ghost-colored cottonwood,
the knot big enough to sit on, frayed,
soft as a little girl's hair. As it slides past,
even the water knows—we've been here
before. These things happen.

MY NAME

Why won't they speak it—
the flute of them,
the drum—
Why not say nothing but!
Aren't they worthy?
Aren't they funny
enough, in their thin skins,
jigging those breakable
bones I made
them, gazing up
intent and erroneous
through impossible jelly eyes?
Seriously, they worry about
pronunciation? Let me just say
I could use a good laugh.
I've got to get through
another day on Earth
among their kind! As if my name's
a skull and crossbones, a bullying
thundercloud coming, but it's just
a syllable, slight jot, and what
does avoiding it do?
Are they afraid their children
once started won't
be able to stop?

GOD CONTEMPLATES THE QUESTION: "IF YOU WERE AN ANIMAL"

A tortoise, full of eggs and slowness, or
a buffalo lumbering or the laden bee,
legs heavy with bee-bread pulling her down.
My hands the rays of the replicating starfish
and your question is the cause.

Or I'm the stubborn, slow-dug nest
and the future still a long scrabble to the sea.
What's my choice? Surge into it and live
or die in the sand with my sisters,
either way leaving no story, no name.

GOD'S IMPOTENCE

I've never lost it—yet—well started
to once but the phone rang and mercifully
she thought it was her sister so she
got up to answer it and by the time
she got back I was halfway hard again
and she wasn't in the mood anyway because
it wasn't her sister it was her mother but
my god I've been avoiding her sometimes
out of fear it'll happen again.

We used to like it in the afternoon
we had forever but that was before
everyone started putting their feet up
before the invention of answering
machines and voicemail and worrying
what everyone's up to forgetting that
this particular infinity's running out
storm rising in the west maybe one
last chance to get laid before
the end of civilization and sleep.

CRAVING SOLITUDE

the prayers
of such company
keen as combine blades
what if   no trace   a long tingling

trail   down space   I mean no
harm to anyone no   suffering
but I thirst I want   my former
void no secrecy   no edges

be only sound
curling on a skin
of water motion   stilled
my only child   startled silence

sailing light   and light   and light
I'd heel   this craft   on its side
through the repeating dark sling
the rope out and go

WITH SAINT PETER AT THE GATE

Not her. No more tonight.
I read the header from my curb:
Housewife Bombs Clinic.

But while she barged downtown,
the babysitter was feeling up
her daughter in the den, her son

fingering backissues of *Jugs* his dad
keeps hidden in the shed. She dumped
the stray cat across town

when the kids were at school, did I
tell you that? Her husband nightly
singed by her disgust though his

love is 87% clean, about as good as it gets. Let
her cool those size six heels. Can't we just
lose her number—no, wait—

say she writes *bitch* a hundred
trillion times. Or this'll get her.
Free love. Make her write it again and again.

GOD GOES TO CONFESSION

It's been ninety-eight years since my last confession, but
I'm up to thirty-nine thousand, one hundred and seven
hail-Marys on account, so—
Watching the other planets, a little down time. After that war,
had to get away… I know: I got through Genghis,
Charlemagne, fleets of fratricidal fiascos, so why now?
The ingenious machinery of it all, the—

All right: I should have stayed, tried
to help with what came after, the evil
mustache of that homunculus with the ovens.
But don't you remember the prayers went stale,
the know-it-all soliloquies on all sides? And their questions!
The Buddhists were good, but they weren't talking to me.
I took a sabbatical. Everyone does it, they—

One: indifference. Two: thirst
to move on. Three: lack of love because love
was difficult. Four? I forgot
my higher power? I slung in space
to watch Pluto, turning like a juicy orange
in the blueblack currents of night.
I tuned my ears to the chime

of Saturn's rings, jingling like old wheels.
Mars, the lumpen peaceful one, but Rover
criss-crossing reminded me of home.
So I'd scoot off to Jupiter for soothing,
brood on her inexplicable spot, her
swirls of mystery. I hovered disconnected,
disaffected, dis—

But I couldn't come back. All the flinches
of PTSD and then some. I had to figure out
why I'd started, forgive myself my
disasters. It helped that I began to wonder who
made those other worlds and how they
felt about it now, their creations spinning
loose, consequencing, free.

GOD KICKING HIMSELF ONE MORE TIME

if there hadn't been seven days
if water hadn't answered light

if man had lain as still as stone if atoms
had not whirled nor woman

taken pity on form if the gates
hadn't held if they'd lacked the courage

if they hadn't loved the feel of words
if the milk of their breasts had forgotten

if the children hadn't been one and another
if monkeys had beaten them down to extinction

or horses carried them over the cliffs
if fur had not felt so good against skin and

money never appeared from hands
if symbols could return the favor or stories

be real before they were told
if I'd never started this

if I were allowed to help them now
if I hadn't run out of time

HEAVEN

Kept thinking I knew how to fit in finally
with your plans, the way you think down there,
but what I had pictured was a party, bon
voyage, favorite people, foods, trees, the grass

salvation-sweet, sky liberty-blue, the can-can
in your blood an orange rejoicing, forgiveness
abundant as potato chips, lust's pincers
gone, greed's shackles clanked open, regret

just a story where you finally get the punchline.
Your true love and your other true love and your other
true love all unite in remembering your charms,
your mother there the way she could have grown to be if

things in her life had been different, and you
can take it all in, down to the meat
in the chambers of your bones, the way you knew
all along you could if things had been different: all

of it there: your mind, oasis/blaze the way you knew
and I knew your mind could do it—and it doesn't
matter that for eighty-eight years you didn't pull this off
because you're doing it now, the sudden, perfect

knowledge of your perfect, funny
life—the kiss-ass jobs, unmowed lawns, days you yelled,
complained, blamed your neighbors. Cessation
of crisis, disappointment disbanded, delay dead! That's

the heaven I planned. Only no, your kind,
you do this childish thing, it's got to last, party, party, party;
otherwise you can't believe it's real. Your mind, I mean: you
can't believe it's all in there: everything you need,

your heaven. I thought you'd be ready, see, for the dive
off the end of the board, the scattering of all your borrowed
particles back to quantum multiplicity, the soup
simultaneous / salty / sweet, hot-cold the deep, the dust.

Yes, it's a slash, a crackle, but a blossoming—
Niagara—the rise of dune that blinds the nomads!
You wouldn't believe how good it feels to cease
being that "I," the one you have dragged

everywhere for fear of not existing. You just won't trust
me on this one, will you, no matter what
you mouth in church. But here I am, the only
sustained persistence beyond "beyond,"

assuring you dissolution is superior to "self." You won't
buy it, oh no, because it hasn't happened
to "you," but the only way you get to be
where I am (not) standing today is to take your leap

in ecstasy, kiss your harp-strung mortgaged dinnerparty
of   ego   me   self   ta-ta / goodbye, and ride
over the edge, loving Cain, loving Abel, loving
the unbeing of all you can't imagine yet, and just die.

FREE WILL

Look in their eyes, brown and wonderful—
we didn't have the word mistake yet.
That came later, carving their names,
cutting kindling, then my spectacular

fruit. The one gift they wouldn't
swap... But I believe their deeds run toward
something, though they still fantasize
a future that can't loop back past the toothpaste,

the rocker, broken crocks and latches,
won't boomerang to the crotch of my tree and
split it. They still fight the return to my soil and
how even choice will unbecome.

*

But they add up. I can't explain. When one
vanishes, a gesture's left, a sketch.
It doesn't look like any one of them. Or me.
I'm starting to think it's why I'm here,

to see the current, not the sediment
suspended or the stream.

IV

Castaways

CREATION REMAKE

The air stiffed
itself up like a puff
of egg and surfed off.
Nearing the sea, the air
declaimed: *Time*
for love! Then, taking
a good look at her: *No,*
not for me the growling,
churning, this
chaos. Not exactly stable
yourself, murmured the sea.
Excuse me? Well, look
at you. Mad! Imperfectly
transparent! Four times
your actual size! *At least I*
don't flash myself at the shore
like some cheap—Whoa,
said the sea. I didn't say
unappealing. I approve
of volume. *Oh!* Plus, if you ride
behind and push, we'll really
make waves. Ha ha.
So the air touched
the water, hesitant, then breathed
harder till the crests, courage
over green, started
making light.

LILITH MUCH LATER

God chickened out, I spoke
so plain, then after sweet
Eve, forgot me so
entirely that when we met
much later,
he didn't know me,
not name or face—not even my ghost
history in his smile, but the usual
party questions... where I lived...
what I grew... did I have a cat?
The strangest
liberation—could have
left it at that. Still,
there was something...
that I alone remember
how his bones keened
and blistered as he tore me
into being. I lay with him
in the back garden after the others
left. I held him when
he cried, still not guessing why,
the big lunk. He thanked me
next dawn for the sympathy, not
knowing what it cost.

AND SHE FOR THE GOD IN HIM

We landed, and the trees as I recall
made the green light a veil of safety
across the highest boughs.
I needed that kindness of leaves

once I had truly seen him. How spit
flecked his lips, how he thrust thick
steps, barking *Bitchcuntwhore.*
Look what you made me do.

Look what you did! Because
of his raving, because he
would not take some blame, the gate
was nailed. *Be strong for him, wait,*

God said. But he stamped and postured
on the shore. I would not be his cure
or keeper, but another seeker (and as
stubborn): my apple, my door.

BETTY FRIEDAN READS TO EVE WHO'S SICK IN BED

So he wanted you to wash down in the crook
of knees, caves between toes, scour the stove and
under your shoes. Peel the veneer off the old table
and relaminate with someone better, at least
someone new. He wanted a cloud, a closet,

a harvest of tea. It finally didn't mean much.
Last month it was higher heels, better grade
of hamburg, softer name, one to mystify
or at least make other guys jealous. You got him those
things, and the previous list: louder,

shorter, in red, no, pink, then black with no jewelry
or hose. The score was too largo, swollen, then too much
pizzicato on the strings! You became whatever, so he lost
you, now he's mad. He thinks there's not enough
of you. Today you see: that's not it at all.

AGING EVE

There should have been other hands
at work. I know something better could
have unfolded from the core of my quickly
mortal body. By sixty I lived where the tree
scattered fruit in my yard. The sea that blue

the wearer never tires of, the sea a simple,
repeating idea, that by now I ought to be free.
I think of the child, fruit of the fruit of my life,
and hope I'll never feel again such shining
ache in my arms, for if I do,

I'll dream again the long knife used
to chop back the tough, tall grasses of the yard,
knife the girl next door, businesslike and happy,
taught me to sharpen with a stone. My wings,
if my god had picked me, would have had

feathers like the long petals of magnolia,
like flesh from lungs of foals born
knowing how to gallop, my wings safe
in the unsafe morning, muscled, opening
over a world just waiting to be claimed.

MARY'S RETURN

So I take back the lost
province my body
from the clamor of silence

this body I gave
to make him then he

wasted it like trash I
take it all back punting
my dear boat of sorrows

solid again I enter towing
my body on its long tough tether

nothing monstrous
can touch it the only
danger ever has been love

ADVERB GOD

a question a door   we pass very
   through continual   stealthily   smelling of rebellion
under three sly crows   like rain   belatedly
   contentedly   within   when the meat has spoiled
riding on empty   during driest sorrow
   up the chute   the throat the tune

when all else fails

with self-pitying step   and sometimes / often
   sweetly   in bitterness broad
as breath flowers in the cold   humming
   without a single doubt   in the world   rhythmically
if we are lucky   too and   soon
   into the slitted   eye

LILITH TO P.O.S.S.L.Q.

Well, yeah, Clinton's dick was
small. Maybe to your face
we lie to soothe, but later
roll our eyes. "Size does not
matter," true—but when
you are small just say it:
no stallion or mast or even
state-fair root vegetable,
but a guy, with your
guy stuff, which is fine
if you pay attention.
Under the executive
desk with basic dark of thighs
around him, he didn't see
her, or that she couldn't
tell it's his cigar. You heard
rumors Hillary liked biker
chicks? Wouldn't you, married
to Little Will, Preoccupied Prez,
bound to another Bill the Blind?

ON THE MAGDALENE'S HAND
A ROUGHENED SPOT

the title's   scratched away but
the syllables   the voice is real
and calls to him   my judge
my ear my child   my final
target   he turned away
yet I am well   will he return
answer yes I   feel he will
among us   a tide pulls
hard a line   around us signals
but what!   where/however/if
the story's told   until we hear it set it
forth not askew   lose all taste for bitterness also
for the sugar-easy   someone will climb
the next hill hear a bell   and suggest a word
someone returns returns and   returns ringing

MARTHA ANSWERS

How did I come back when
everything tasted like coal? When
my own sister could go
to the funeral, bent white
bud in her buttonhole, and not
see me sitting one row over?
How, when the food I cooked, if
I cooked, tasted like the pan?
The way back, I couldn't tell you,
or the scenery or the boat. I think
you already know anyway, but
when it was me, I dreamed the ocean,
its rise and fall and
rise and we were
its burden and its eye.
Somehow comforted, somehow
the sound of a truck engine
winding up the valley stopped
hurting. I started running again.
Kept going, feet like strangers,
sweat breaking, I came on, still
afraid of dying, but I could feel
the shudder under my ribs again
and had no mercy and made it go on.

LUCIFER

Do you know, by his side I had forgotten?
Invisible hands have the job: to part us
from our dear flesh, slowly.
       His walled garden,
the little traps: siren voices of the flowers
and the moon to cut us open.
       I'm done needing
someone to agree with me, to nod, to say my name.
The tiny shedding feathers of the eye…
       What knowledge
costs. My hair ribboned white scatters ash where I go,
the skin opens to take more of the fire he sends.
No more resistance.
       I am done with him.
As close as this to
myself and as clear and distant (—what
once I was!—) till now I have not been.

EVE (REPRISE)

I passed jam you did not ask for
and you started getting mad.
But look: this time God's out
gathering useless, beautiful
horse chestnuts, fat leeches latched on
up to his knees, letting them feed
and getting easy and easy
in that godskin. Oh, so perforated
we are now and still
we cannot bend? I give up
helping you out of the bath
you never wanted anyway.
The answers turn
out to be selfish as leeches,
clean as God lying
flat in the sun, un-
harmable. There's the whistle,
calling. You know it's true.

RUTH REMEMBERS

Honey, you know how it goes:
what doesn't kill you...
You've got ghosts, I've
got ghosts—Oh, my wedding cup
was all over garnets. The little pops
of light, that was mica
in the clay. God put me
in some unlikely places and he said
grow. Just another tumbled
rock on shore, rounder and
rounder. What's a life anyhow
but sense enough for one?
And then, sometime, it ends.
And what was yours was yours.

NOTES

"Noa": One of the five daughters of Zelophehad who successfully petitioned Moses to persuade God to allow women to inherit (if they had no brothers). The name is still in use, but even so is unfamiliar to many.

"On Setting Her Free": The speaker here is Judith, famous for her conquest of the general Holofernes. After seducing him, she cuts off his head and delivers it to the elders of her village who had been planning to surrender rather than fight. Judith was accompanied by "her maid," who is given no name but is mentioned numerous times.

"God Awoke in the Garden," "Lilith Much Later," and "Lilith to P.O.S.S.L.Q": Lilith is sometimes defined as a demon, sometimes seen as God's first draft before [H]e created Eve. Either way, she was trouble and cast aside.

ACKNOWLEDGMENTS

Many thanks to the editors who published poems from this collection in the following journals:

Artful Dodge: "Neighbor"
Bryant Literary Review: "New in Town"
Caveat Lector: "On Setting Her Free"
Cider Press Review: "Lilith to P.O.S.S.L.Q."
Confrontation: "God Awoke in the Garden" & "To Esther"
Diner: "Aging Eve" (as "The Other Eve")
Faultline: "Applicant"
Field: "Lucifer" & "Eve: Reprise"
Fugue: "Look Up"
Harpur Palate: "Ruth Remembers"
New Orleans Review: "Christ Explains His Youth"
Nimrod: "Noah" & "Creation Remake"
Off the Coast: "Holofernes" & "Rebeka"
Phoebe: "Ruth to Her Daughter"
Pine Hills Review: "Martha Admits She Was Angry"
Puerto del Sol: "Adverb God"
Seneca Review: "Heaven"
Sojourners: "Disciple, Tangiers"
Stand: "Magdalene" (as "Ordinary")
The Literary Review: "Between Testaments"
The Pinch: "Ruth at the Well"

More Poetry from Tiger Bark Press

Pricking, by Jessica Cuello
Dinner with Emerson, by Wendy Mnookin
As Long As We Are Not Alone, by Israel Emiot, trans. Leah Zazulyer
Be Quiet, by Kuno Raeber, trans. Stuart Friebert
Psalter, by Georgia Popoff
Slow Mountain Train, by Roger Greenwald
The Burning Door, by Tony Leuzzi
I've Come This Far to Say Hello: Poems Selected and New, by Kurt Brown
After That, by Kathleen Aguero
Crossing the Yellow River, trans. Sam Hamill
Night Garden, by Judith Harris
Time~Bound, by Kurt Brown
Sweet Weight, by Kate Lynn Hibbard
The Gate at Visby, by Deena Linett
River of Glass, by Ann McGovern
Inside Such Darkness, by Virginia Slachman
Transfiguration Begins at Home, by Estha Weiner
The Solvay Process, by Martin Walls
A Pilgrim into Silence, by Karen Swenson